# PLAY THE GAME

# JUDO

## JUSTIN DANDO

BLANDFORD

First published in Great Britain in 1990
by Ward Lock. Reprinted 1991.
Revised by Blandford 1993.
A Cassell imprint.

Designed by Anita Ruddell
Illustrations by James G. Robins

Text set in Helvetica
by Hourds Typographica, Stafford, England
Printed in England by The Bath Press, Avon

**British Library Cataloguing in Publication Data**
Dando, Justin
  Judo. — (Play the game)
  1. Judo — Manuals
  I. Title   II. Series
  796.8'152
  ISBN 0 7137 24161

# *Acknowledgments*

The publishers would like to thank Allsport
UK Ltd for supplying the pictures on pages
9, 24/25, 37, 56 and Colorsport for those on
pages 2, 12/13, 17, 20, 29 and 49.

**Frontispiece:**
**Peter Seisenbacher of Austria (left) and**
**Kim Seung-Kyu of South Korea in**
**Olympic action.**

# CONTENTS

# FOREWORD

I am delighted to see that Ward Lock have included judo as one of the titles in their *Play the Game* series. The number of newcomers to judo increases every year and consequently they need a firm base on which to start their development.

Through the British Judo Association we have many capable coaches up and down the country who provide assistance but we feel that *Play the Game: Judo* is a very good starting point for anybody either thinking about taking up the sport, or who has just started and needs to check out the basics of judo.

The book provides an excellent insight into the history of our sport and explains the rules, equipment and terminology. And in the game judo there is a lot of that which, to the newcomer, sounds foreign . . .that's because it is – Japanese! But *Play the Game* translates the every-day judo terms so that the novice can get to grips with the terminology, which is almost as important as being able to perfect the throws and holds.

The technique section also gives an insight into the holds and throws that will be encountered in the early stage of one's development.

Judo is a sport enjoyed by millions; and age and sex are no barrier. I am confident that once you have spent your first day in a judo club you will be looking forward to your next visit. But between visits, you can do a lot worse than sitting down and reading *Play the Game: Judo.*

**Michael Leigh**
*Chairman*
*British Judo Association*

# HISTORY &
# DEVELOPMENT OF
# JUDO

**J**udo is an exciting unarmed combat sport that originated in the Orient as a means of self-defence which has since grown into an international competitive sport.

Judo developed out of ju-jitsu, a form of unarmed combat believed to have been introduced into Japan by a Chinese monk, Chen Yuan-ping in the early seventeenth century. Various ju-jitsu schools developed and young *samurai* were instructed in the art. This was in the days of chivalry among Japanese knights.

*Samurai* warriors carried swords as a form of armed combat and also used ju-jitsu with lethal effect. However, in 1871 the *samurai* were forbidden to carry swords but they continued to use ju-jitsu lethally and it brought the art into disrepute.

The skills of unarmed combat were saved by Dr Jigoro Kano who studied at various ju-jitsu schools. He brought together the best techniques of each to develop his own style, introducing it at his school. He called the style *Kodokan Judo*. He formed a principle which ju-jitsu had also earlier discovered – *tskuri-komi*, the art of getting a fighter off balance before throwing him, Kano

described the difference between judo and ju-jitsu as: 'the elevation of an art to a principle.'

In studying judo he felt it was necessary to train the body, essential in all forms of martial arts. But just as importantly, he saw the need to develop the mind. 'Maximum efficiency with minimum effort', was a Kano belief.

The Kodokan was founded in 1882 but was slow to establish itself as one of the leading schools because there still remained an interest in ju-jitsu. But, in 1886, the Kodokan and the Totsuka, the biggest ju-jitsu school, took part in a competition organized by the Tokyo Metropolitan Police Board. Each school fielded a 15-man team and the Kodokan won 13 contests with the other two being drawn. From that day, the popularity of judo increased while that of ju-jitsu declined.

However, Kano wanted to spread the word of judo beyond Japan and in 1889 he visited Europe taking with him the leading judo exponent Yukio Tani, who gave the first display in Britain. At the turn of the century, Yamashita, another Kano pupil, started giving instructions in the United States. He

# JUDO

even taught the sport to President Theodore Roosevelt.

The Paris police were taught judo as a form of self-defence and Yukio Tani established himself as a great music hall act. He would take on, and often beat, the professional wrestlers of the day who were star attractions.

Europe's first judo club was not formed until 1918 when Gunji Koizumi opened the famous Budokwai in Westminster, London. The club's first instructor was Tani who would often drive his pupils to near despair with his intense schedules.

The first international judo match took place in 1926 when the Budokwai beat the German national team. The sport spread to Australia in 1928 thanks to Shinzo Tagaki, another of Kano's star pupils, and in 1929 he took judo to India. Two years later it was introduced into Africa. In the 1930s, many European experts travelled to Japan to learn techniques and the first Briton to make the trip was Trevor Leggett in 1938.

Despite judo's spread across the continents, it was still looked upon as a means of self-defence rather than a sport. It was not until after the Second World War that it developed into a competitive sport.

The European Judo Union was founded in 1948, as was the British Judo Association. It was not until 1951, however, that the International Judo Federation was formed.

The European Championship was the first major international event. First held at the Royal Albert Hall in 1951, it subsequently became an annual fixture. The British, Dutch and French dominated the early championships. But the Japanese stole the first World Championships in Tokyo in 1956 when Shokichi Natsui took the first prize. His fellow countryman Yasuji Sone won the title two years later. When the championships were held in Paris in 1961 the giant Dutchman Anton Geesink showed that the gap between the Japanese and the rest of the world had narrowed when he beat three Japanese fighters on his way to taking the title.

At that time there was only an Open class of competition because the judo belief always maintained that a big man could always be beaten by a smaller man of equal skill. But Geesink was an 18 stone, 6'6" giant who was also skilful. His arrival brought about the introduction of weight classes.

With Tokyo hosting the 1964 Olympics they requested that the IOC include the sport in the programme for the first time. This duly happened and Geesink won the Open category gold medal. Japanese fighters won the other three weight-division gold medals that were at stake.

While the Open category remains in most competitions, it is invariably won by a heavyweight, which highlights how power and strength play an important part in judo these days.

Women, too, compete at international level. The Women's World Championship was introduced in 1980 and was included as a demonstration sport at the 1988 Seoul Olympics. They will be competing for the first time at the 1992 Olympics.

The Soviets have proved to be a threat to the top Japanese and leading western European fighters in recent years. They have developed their own style of judo which stems from their sambo style – a cross between judo and wrestling.

Judo extends beyond the realms of top class international competition. It is very popular outside the competitive arena and men, women and children find they can benefit from judo which, if practiced on a less competitive level, has a good aesthetic value. Age is no barrier to judo either. Youngsters and older people alike can enjoy the sport. The British Judo Association encourages children to take it up and issues a guide to the grading syllabus for boys and girls between the ages of 8 and 15. You're never too young, or old, to take up judo.

**Belgium's Ingrid Berghmans (right) was one of the most dominant figures in ladies judo in the 1980s**

# EQUIPMENT & TERMINOLOGY

**B**efore starting to learn how to play judo, it is important to familiarize yourself with the equipment needed, and the terminology you will come across as you get to grips with the sport.

## EQUIPMENT

Judo is far from an expensive sport to take up. The basic equipment consists of a padded mat and, for the individual, a white suit (known as the *judogi*) consisting of a

loose fitting top and trousers with no buttons or pockets. The loose fitting nature of the clothing is essential to the many skills involved in judo. The jacket must be long enough to cover the hips, the sleeves must cover at least half of the forearm, and the trousers should cover half of the lower leg.

Because of the violent nature of some of the grips and throws, the stitching is extra strong, particularly around the lapels and armpits. The jacket should be securely fastened using the belt (non-buckle type) and it should be doubly wrapped around the waist and tied as shown so as to prevent it coming undone during a contest. Shoes are not worn.

Membership to a club is essential and again the charge is not excessive. If you are fortunate enough to have a choice when choosing a club, you should enquire whether you, as a novice, along with other novices, will get special treatment. It is pointless joining a club that sees you pitched in with other experienced fighters right from the start. That will do nothing to help your development. Also make sure that the club has a good training programme for the newcomer and enquire if they have insurance cover. If not, you are well advised to take out separate cover against personal injury. It won't cost much but could be worth it in the long term.

To secure the jacket make sure the belt is long enough to be
wrapped around your waist twice.
Take the two ends around your back.
Bring them back to the front.

Cross them.
Pass the end in your right hand under the belt close to the body.

Make a knot with the end that is in your left hand.
Pull tightly to secure the knot.

All fighters, known as *judoka*, are graded according to skill and the two senior grades are **Kyu** (pronounced 'Q') for the pupil and **Dan** for the more experienced fighters. However, there is also a **Mon** grade for junior boys and girls between the ages of 8 and 15. All wear belts and are coloured according to status. The full list is as follows:

**1st Mon** White belt with one $\frac{1}{2}$in red bar

**2nd Mon** White belt with two $\frac{1}{2}$in red bars

**3rd Mon** White belt with three $\frac{1}{2}$in red bars

**4th Mon** Yellow belt with one $\frac{1}{2}$in red bar

**5th Mon** Yellow belt with two $\frac{1}{2}$in red bars

**6th Mon** Yellow belt with three $\frac{1}{2}$in red bars

**7th Mon** Orange belt with one $\frac{1}{2}$in red bar

**8th Mon** Orange belt with two $\frac{1}{2}$in red bars

**9th Mon** Orange belt with three $\frac{1}{2}$in red bars

**10th Mon** Green belt with one $\frac{1}{2}$in red bar

**11th Mon** Green belt with two $\frac{1}{2}$in red bars

**12th Mon** Green belt with three $\frac{1}{2}$in red bars

**13th Mon** Blue belt with one $\frac{1}{2}$in red bar

**14th Mon** Blue belt with two $\frac{1}{2}$in red bars

**15th Mon** Blue belt with three $\frac{1}{2}$in red bars

**16th Mon** Brown belt with one $\frac{1}{2}$in red bar

(*list is continued overleaf*)

**Brian Jacks did much to raise the profile of Judo in britain. He is seen here against Shinobu Sekine of Japan at the 1972 Munich Olympics. Sekine won the middleweight gold, and Jacks took one of the bronze medals**

# JUDO

| 17th Mon | Brown belt with two ½in red bars |
| 18th Mon | Brown belt with three ½in red bars |
| 9th Kyu | Yellow belt |
| 8th Kyu | Orange belt |
| 7th Kyu | Orange belt |
| 6th Kyu | Green belt |
| 5th Kyu | Green belt |
| 4th Kyu | Blue belt |
| 3rd Kyu | Blue belt |
| 2nd Kyu | Brown belt |
| 4th Dan | Black belt |
| 5th Dan | Black belt |
| 6th Dan | Red and White belt |
| 7th Dan | Red and White belt |
| 8th Dan | Red and White belt |
| 9th Dan | Red belt |
| 10th Dan | Red belt |
| 11th Dan | Red belt |
| 12th Dan | White belt |

Fighting ability and technical knowledge can take you to 5th Dan. Thereafter, advancement depends on service to the sport. While it is possible to reach 12th Dan, this has never been achieved and the highest grade ever awarded by the Kodokan is 10th Dan.

Gradings played an important role in judo in its early days but have a less important role these days. However, they still act as a guideline to a person's individual standard and capabilities.

## The mat

The mat, known as the *tatami*, comprises a 10m (33ft) square area with a 1m (3ft) danger area around the perimeter, and a 1m (3ft) safety area surrounding the entire contest area.

The area can be made up of a single, straw-filled mat, covered in a tightly stretched canvas, or of a series of smaller mats closely pushed together to make the required 10m (33ft) square area.

# *TERMINOLOGY*

Most of the technology in judo is of Japanese origin and, while it may sound strange at first, you will soon pick it up and find yourself using the Japanese terms rather than their English translations. Those terms printed in **bold** are covered in detail later in the book.

***Ashi-waza*** Collective name for throws made by the foot and leg. The following are all forms of ashi-waza:

| *ashi-guruma* | – leg wheel |
| *deashi-barai* | – foot sweep |
| *harai-tsurikomi-ashi* | – sweeping ankle draw |
| *hiza guruma* | – knee wheel |
| *ko-soto-gake* | – minor outer hook |
| ***ko-soto-gari*** | – minor outer reaping |
| ***ko-uchi-gari*** | – minor inner reaping |
| *o-guruma* | – major wheel |
| ***okuri-ashi-barai*** | – sliding ankle sweep |
| ***o-soto-gari*** | – major outer reaping |
| *o-soto-guruma* | – major outer wheel |

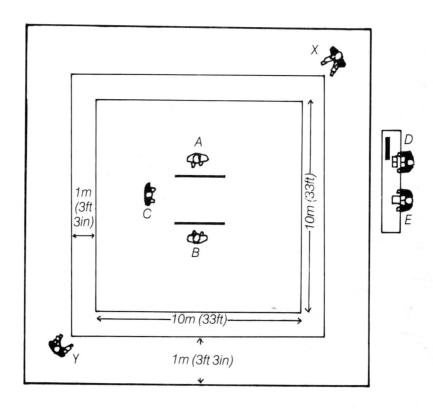

The mat and surrounding area. The mat is usually made up of smaller mats pushed together to make a 9m (30ft) square area. There is a 1m (3ft) border surrounding the main mat. This should either be a different coloured matting c  be clearly marked in another colour to indicate it is a danger area. Around the perimeter there is a safety area which is a minimum of 3m (10ft) from the danger area.

The two contestants take up positions at A and B before each contest and the two judges are positioned diagonally opposite each other at X and Y.

The referee C must start facing (D) and (E) and thereafter will adopt a roving position.

Two officials, a scorer (D) and timekeeper (E), sit at a table well away from the safety area.

# JUDO

**o-uchi-gari** — major inner reaping

**sasae-tsurikomi-ashi** — propping drawing ankle

**uchi-mata** — inner thigh reaping

**Chui** A referee's call to note a serious infringement. It is a yuko score.

**Dan** A degree of competence.

**Dojo** A training hall.

**Gyaku** Means 'reverse' when applied to locks, holds, etc.

**Hadake-jime** A strangle.

**Hajime** The referee's call to 'begin' the contest.

**Hansoku-make** The referee's call to indicate a disqualification.

**Hantei** The referee's call to indicate a decision is required from the judges.

**Harai-goshi** A sweeping hip throw.

*The effect of Harai-goshi*

**Hiki-wake** The referee's call to indicate a drawn match in a team contest.

**Ippon** The call of the referee to indicate that the perfect throw (10 points) has been scored. It is called if a fighter has: (a) made the perfect throw by throwing his opponent cleanly and directly onto his back; (b) has held his opponent onto the mat for 30 seconds, or (c) gained a submission.

**Ippon-seoi-nage** A one-arm shoulder throw of an opponent onto his back.

**Jigotai** The adopting of a defensive posture.

**Judogi** The judo costume.

**Judoka** A person who practices judo.

**Juji-gatame** A cross-arm lock hold.

**Juji-jime** A cross-arm strangle grip.

**Ju-no-kata** The demonstration of forms of gentleness.

**Kaeshiwaza** Counter-attacking techniques.

**Kami-shiho-gatame** A grappling technique trapping the upper four quarters.

**Kansetsu-waza** Arm-locks. The following are all *kansetsu-waza*:

**hiza-gatame** – knee arm-lock
**juji-gatame** – cross arm-lock
**ude-garami** – entangled arm-lock
**ude-gatame** – arm crush
**waki-gatame** – armpit arm-lock

**Kata** Literally translated as form, some basic techniques are not included in the seven traditional kata.

**Kata-gatame** A method of shoulder holding.

**Neil Adams (right) won silver medals at both the 1980 Moscow and 1984 Los Angeles Games.**

**Kata-ha-jime**　A neck-lock.

**Katame-waza**　Collective name for groundwork techniques. The following are the three forms of *katame-waza*:

 kansetsu-waza – arm-locks
 osae-komi-waza– hold-down techniques
 shime-waza  – stranglehold techniques

**Keikoku**　A referee's call indicating a warning against a participant for a grave infringement. A seven-point penalty is also awarded against the guilty *judoka*.

**Kesa-gatame**　A scarf-hold.

**Koka**　The referee's call to indicate a three-point score.

**Koshi-waza**　Description of hip throw techniques. The following are all *koshi-waza*:

 hane-goshi  – spring hip throw
 **harai-goshi**  – sweeping loin throw
 koshi-guruma – hip wheel throw
 **o-goshi**   – major hip throw
 suki-nage  – scooping throw
 tsuri-goshi  – lifting hip throw
 **tsuri-komi-goshi**– lift pull hip throw
 uki-goshi  – floating hip throw
 ushiro goshi – rear hip throw
 utsuri-goshi – changing hip throw

# JUDO

**Ko-soto-gake**  Minor outside-leg block.

**Ko-soto-gari**  Minor outer reaping leg throw.

**Ko-uchi-gari**  Minor inner reaping leg throw.

**Kyu**  A pupil grade.

**Makikomi**  A winding throw.

**Ma-sutemi-waza**  Name used to describe rear sacrifice techniques. The following are all *ma-sutemi-waza*:

   *sumi-gaeshi* – corner throw
   **tomoe-nage** – stomach throw
   *ura-nage*    – rear throw

**Matte**  The referee's call to wait as the contest is temporarily stopped.

**Morote-gari**  Two-handed scoop. A throw made by grasping behind the opponent's knees with both hands and scooping him backwards.

**Morote-seoi-nage**  A double-arm shoulder throw.

*Morote-seoi-nage*

**Nage-waza**  Collective name for standing techniques. The following are all *nage-waza*:

   *ashi-waza* – foot and leg techniques
   *koshi-waza* – hip techniques
   *te-waza*    – hand techniques

**Newaza**  Groundwork done in order to gain an advantage by a series of moves, counter-moves and feints.

**O-goshi**  An over-the-hip throw.

*O-goshi*

**Okuri-ashi-barai**  A sliding ankle sweep.

**Okuri-eri-jime**  A strangle.

**Osae-komi**  The referee's call to indicate 'holding'.

**Osae-komi-waza**  Used to describe hold-down techniques. The following are all forms of *osae-komi-waza*:

   **kami-shiho-gatame** – upper four quarter hold
   **kata-gatame** – shoulder hold
   **kesa-gatame** – scarf hold
   **tate-shiho-gatame** – trunk hold

*Yoko-shiho-gatame*

**ushiro-kesa-gatame** – reverse scarf hold
**yoko-shiho-gatame** – side four quarter hold

**O-soto-gake**   Major outside-leg block throw.

**O-soto-gari**   Major outside-leg reaping throw.

**O-uchi-gake**   Major inside-leg block throw.

**O-uchi-gari**   Major inner reaping leg throw.

**Randori**   Practise with a colleague but without the pressure of a competitive situation.

**Reaping**   Using the back of the foot and leg to perfect a throw.

**Renraku-waza**   A series of combination techniques.

**Sasae-tsurikomi-ashi**   Propping drawing ankle.

**Scarf**   A grappling technique with your arm(s) around the back of your opponent's neck – hence the name.

**Sensei**   A judo teacher.

**Seoi-nage**   A shoulder throw.

**Seoi-otoshi**   A shoulder drop.

**Shiai**   A judo contest.

**Shido**   A referee's call indicating an infringement, with a koka penalty.

*Shido*

**Shihan**   The judo master.

**Shime-waza**   Description of stranglehold techniques. The following are all *shime-waza*:

*gyaku-juji-jime* – reverse cross lock
**hadake-jime**   – naked choke strangle
**kata-ha-jime**   – single wing strangle
*kata-juji-jime*   – half cross strangle
**nami-juji-jime** – normal cross strangle
**okuri-eri-jime** – sliding collar strangle
*tomoe-jime*   – circular strangle
*tsukikomi-jime* – thrusting choke

*Sono-mama*

**Sono-mama**   The referee's call telling the contestants to 'freeze' and not move.

**Sore-made**   The referee's call indicating that that is the end.

**Sutemi-waza**   Collective name for sacrifice techniques. The two forms of *sutemi-waza* are: *ma-sutemi-waza* (rear sacrifice techniques) and *yoko-sutemi-waza* (side sacrifice techniques).

**Tachi-waza**   Name given to the standing techniques. The following are all *tachi-waza*:

**ippon-seoi-nage**   – one-arm shoulder throw
*kate-guruma*   – shoulder wheel
**morote-seoi-nage** – two-arm shoulder throw
**morote-seoi-otoshi**– shoulder drop
*sumi-otoshi*   – corner drop
**tai-otoshi**   – body drop
*uko-otoshi*   – floating drop

*Hadake-jime*

**Britain's Keith Remfry (left) on his way to an Olympic silver medal.**

**Tai-otoshi**   A forward throw with the legs astride.

**Tani-otoshi**   Known as the 'Valley Drop' it is performed by sitting down using one of your legs to block your opponent's legs.

Grip your opponent's ribs when performing *Tate-shiho-gatame*

The opening move of *Uchi-mata*.

**Tate-shiho-gatame** A lengthwise hold by straddling your opponent.

**Te-guruma** A hand wheel – a throw by lifting your opponent off the ground by his upper thigh.

**Te-waza** Name given to hand techniques before effecting a throw. For details of throws see *Tachi-waza*.

**Toketa** The referee's call to indicate a fighter has broken from a hold.

**Tomoe-nage** A stomach throw.

**Tsuri-komi-ashi** A throw utilizing the ankle.

**Tsuri-komi-goshi** A lift-pull hip throw achieved by first getting your opponent off balance.

**Uchi-komi** Forcing an opponent off balance without completing the movement. Used as a training technique.

**Uchi-mata** An inner thigh throw.

# EQUIPMENT · & · TERMINOLOGY

*Ude-gatame*

**Ude-garami**  An entangled arm-lock form of grappling.

**Ude-gatame**  A straight arm-lock hold.

**Ukemi**  A means of breaking the fall.

**Ushiro-kesa-gatame**  A reverse scarf hold.

**Waki-gatame**  An arm-pit hold.

Locking the elbow joint in *Waki-gatame*

Diane Bell won the half-middleweight world title in 1986

Waza-ari

**Yoko-sutemi-waza** Name given to side sacrifice techniques. The following are all *yoko-sutemi-waza*:

| | |
|---|---|
| *hane-makikomi* | – winding spring hip |
| **tani-otoshi** | – valley drop |
| *uki-waza* | – floating throw |
| *yoko-gake* | – side dash |
| *yoko-guruma* | – side wheel |
| *yoko-otoshi* | – side drop |
| *yoko-wakare* | – side separation |

Yoshi

**Waza** Technique.

**Waza-ari** Referee's call to indicate the throw is not as definite as the *ippon* and the competitor has not landed completely on his back. The *waza-ari* is known as 'almost a point' and is worth seven points. Scored with a hold of more than 25 but less than 30 seconds.

**Waza-ari-awasete-ippon** A seven-point score added to another seven-point score to give an *ippon*.

**Yoko-shiho-gatame** A grappling technique using the side four quarters.

**Yoshi** The referee's call to 'carry on' or 'continue'.

**Yuko** The referee's call to indicate a five-point score.

Yoko-shiho-gatame

**Tani-otoshi**

*Another sutemi-waza, or sacrifice technique, known as the Valley drop. After pulling the opponent from a right-side posture to break balance and force a step backwards, follow this more and push on the left lapel whilst pulling downwards and backwards on the right sleeve. Lower your hips and slide left leg onto the mat by your opponent's foot, as shown here. Drop your opponent over your outstretched legs.*

# THE GAME – A GUIDE

Judo can simply be described as a form of wrestling. You have to get your opponent down on the mat using one of the many throws available, all of which are capable of scoring points. Alternatively, you can either hold your opponent in position on the mat for a prescribed period of time, or gain a submission.

That is a simple explanation. But let's now look at the rules of judo in further detail.

At one time all judo contests were in an Open category. But since the introduction of weight limits, only fighters from within one weight limit will fight another. However, the Open class still exists, but, more often than not, supremacy will be with the heavier fighter.

At international level the following weight categories exist for men and women:

| Men | Women | |
|-----|-------|---|
| 60kg | 48kg | – extra-lightweight |
| 65kg | 52kg | – half-lightweight |
| 71kg | 56kg | – lightweight |
| 78kg | 61kg | – half-middleweight |
| 86kg | 66kg | – middleweight |
| 95kg | 72kg | – half-heavyweight |
| 95kg + | 72kg + | – heavyweight |
| Any | Any | – open class |

A *shiai* (contest) takes place on a *tatami* (mat). In charge of the contest is a roving referee who keeps a close watch on the action from a position about 2–2.5m (6–8ft) from the fighters. He is assisted by two judges who sit at diagonally opposite corners of the mat. By tradition, the two contestants bow to each other at the commencement and end of a contest.

The length of a contest varies according to the importance of the event but is usually between 2 and 5 minutes, but rarely any longer. Contests in major international events, like the Olympic Games, are unlikely to last longer. Unlike boxing, the contest is not split into rounds. However, a decisive score during the time limit is sufficient to end the contest. If there is no major score at the end of the prescribed time limit the judges will indicate which fighter they believe is the winner. In the event of differing opinions, the referee has the casting vote.

Contests are won by higher scores or by gaining a particular score.

| | |
|---|---|
| *ippon* | – 10 points |
| *waza-ari* | – 7 points |
| *yuko* | – 5 points |
| *koka* | – 3 points |

Thus a victory may be by a yuko or three kokas to two, so let's examine the scoring system.

**One of the game's outstanding fighters, Yasuhiro Yamashita of Japan**

Hajime: *The call to begin. But the referee will only make the call once he is satisfied that everybody is ready and the two contestants have bowed to each other.*

Matte: *The call made to stop the contest. The referee will show his palmed hand to the timekeeper indicating he wants the clock stopping.*

Osae-komi: *Made to indicate a hold has started. The timekeeper will start his clock the moment the referee makes the call.*

Toketa: *Called to indicate a hold has been broken.*

Ippon: *Called to indicate that a maximum ten-point score has been obtained either by a perfect throw, a thirty-second hold, or a submission.*

Waza-ari: *The call to indicate a seven-point score.*

Hantei: *In the case of a drawn contest the refer[ee] will call to the judges to indicate which contesta[nt] they think has won the contest. They give their decision on his call of 'Hantei'.*

# REFEREE'S · SIGNALS

Hike-wake: *The referee's call to indicate a draw.*

Sono-mama: *If the referee calls 'Sono-mama' it is a request for both contestants to freeze or do not move.*

Yoshi: *The call to continue the contest after it has been stopped for a sono-mama call.*

Shido: *The referee's call to the scorer to indicate a slight infringement. He will point to the guilty fighter. Equivalent to awarding a koka to your opponent.*

Chui: *Called if a fighter has commited a serious infringement. Carries a yuko penalty.*

Keikoku: *Another call to indicate an infringement, this time following a grave infringement, which carries a seven-point penalty.*

Hansoku-make: *The call to indicate a fighter has been disqualified. If one fighter commits a very grave infringement, both fighters are returned to their starting positions at the centre of the mat, and the referee faces the guilty fighter and announces 'Hansoku-make'.*

# JUDO

## Ippon

The *ippon* is the maximum score. Once an *ippon* is scored, the contest automatically comes to an end. An *ippon* can be obtained by: (a) completing the perfect throw, (b) holding your opponent for 30 seconds on the mat in the prescribed manner or (c) gaining a submission from an armlock or a strangle.

## Waza-ari

A *waza-ari* is awarded for a near-perfect throw or for a hold of at least 25 seconds but less than 30 seconds. Refereeing judo contests is not easy and the awarding of a *waza-ari* instead of an *ippon*, and vice versa, often causes much controversy. But, in true sporting manner, you must accept the referee's decision as final. The scoring of two *waza-aris*, known as *waza-ari-awasete-ippon*, brings the contest to an end.

## Yuko

Scored when the throw is not quite the value of a *waza-ari*, or if the hold is for more than 20 seconds but less than 25 seconds.

## Koka

A *koka* is called when the throw has not been as effective as the *yuko* and the fighter has landed on his thigh(s) or buttocks with speed or force.

If the contest has not been automatically brought to an end by scoring an *ippon* or *waza-ari-awasete-ippon* then the highest scoring throw will decide the winner. However, points are deducted for infringements, like talking during a contest, employing dangerous or illegal tactics, or moving outside the contest area. The following all carry penalty points:

| | |
|---|---|
| *chui* | – 5 points |
| *keikoku* | – 7 points |
| *hansoku-make* | – 10 points |

Again, let's look at each individually.

## Chui

A caution for a serious infringement of the rules. Carries a yuko penalty.

## Keikoku

A warning for a grave infringement.

## Hansoku-make

The penalty for a very grave infringement. It results in automatic disqualification.

In addition there is one other penalty which the referee can call and that is *shido* which is for a slight infringement. This always awards a score to your opponent.

All the above will be called by the referee and it is worth looking at the signals the referee will make when accompanying each of his calls.

# RULES CLINIC

Right, that's how to 'play' judo. The next chapter will deal with the various throws and holds necessary to score points. But before we go into **Techniques** we will take you through the **Rules Clinic** which will help clear up some of the finer points of the rules which crop up from time-to-time.

**Nothing to do with the rules, I know, but you mentioned that I can get upgraded according to my ability. Is it possible to be downgraded?**

Yes, but suspension from the British Judo Association is far more likely punishment.

**If a fighter has a chui awarded against him and later in the contest receives another similar caution is he disqualified?**

No, but two *chuis* are automatically converted into one *keioku*. Any further penalty results in diqualification.

**How is a decision reached if there hasn't been an ippon?**

OK, let's look at four examples.

*Example 1:* Fighter 'A' has scored a *yuko* (five points) and Fighter 'B' has not scored. Then, as you would imagine, Fighter 'A' is the winner.

*Example 2:* There have been no points scored, and no penalties conceded. So, the contest is awarded to the fighter who the judges believe has been the more aggressive. The judges count the number of attacks and knockdowns.

*Example 3:* Fighter 'A' scores a *waza-ari* but has had a *keikoku* penalty against him. Fighter 'B' has had no points and no penalty points. In this case the winner would be fighter 'B' even though, effectively, both fighers have no points because 'A's total is +7 and −7. Score and penalties are now considered equal and judgement is made on the number of attacks.

*Example 4*: Fighter 'A' has scored three *yukos* (15 points) and fighter 'B' has scored a *waza-ari* (7 points), then player 'B' is the winner because a *waza-ari* is regardad as the more skilful score and therefore beats any number of *yukos*.

**So does example three mean a fighter could have an ippon but lose the contest because he had a 10-point penalty against him as well?**

*You weren't paying attention earlier were you? An ippon* automatically stops a contest, so how could he then have a *hansoku-make* awarded against him? The contest would be over before the penalty.

**When holding down an opponent in order to make a score, apart from the time limits, are there any other regulations concerning the hold?**

Yes, but it not necessary to trap either of your opponents arms in order to make a score. Once any hold has begun the referee will call *osae-komi* (holding) and if the fighter escapes from the hold the referee will call *toketa* (broken).

**In boxing, if fighters get too near the ropes the referee will call for them to 'break' and re-start the action from the middle of the ring. Does this happen in judo if the two fighters get too near the edge of the mat?**

Yes, and no. They aren't asked to break like in boxing. But if they are entwined in a position near the edge of the mat the referee will call *sono-mama* which means 'do not move'. On calling *yoshi* which means 'carry on' or 'continue', the referee will tap both fighters on their bodies at the same time to indicate a resumption in fighting.

Right, that takes care of the rules of judo, now for the all important techniques.

# TECHNIQUE

**S**kill, stamina, fighting spirit and the ability to use your strong points against the weak ones of your opponent are all vital qualities required to make a good *judoka*.

Technique, and the correctness of technique is equally important. You may think you have effected a perfect *ippon* but some flaw in your technique could see the throw downgraded to a *waza-ari*.

The ultimate score is, as we have already seen, the *ippon* and we will look at techniques that will help towards effecting the maximum score. But not all contests are won with an *ippon* and this is where tactics also play an important part of judo. You may well be leading by a slender margin with the end of the contest looming. You are then well advized to go on the defensive. This is the tactical side of the sport.

*Part of judo tradition – the bowing (rei) at both the start and finish of a contest. At the start of a contest the contestants stand alongside their respective mark near to the centre of the mat, carry out the upright bow as a token of respect for the opponent, and take one step over the mark.*

Various holding positions. Note how full use of the jacket is made by both contestants as they attempt to get a good grip using either the lapels, back of the neck, elbows, or cuffs.

**Britain's Dave Starbrook in Olympic action.**

# JUDO

Warming-up with stretching exercises is very important before starting any sport. Judo is no exception. These exercises will help to loosen the back and stomach muscles . . .

*. . . while these will help to loosen up the backs of the legs, thighs and back.* **But be very careful not to overstretch as a serious injury could result.**

Some fighters are specialists at groundwork in that they have particular strengths and skills that are unique to judo when a hold, lock or grapple is being applied. Whilst it is an offence to pull the opponent down in order to start *ne-waza*, this doesn't prevent skilled fighters winning on the mat.

Contests start with the fighters bowing to each other. After that they grapple for position by gripping each other's *judogi* either by the lapels or sleeves as each tries to seek an advantage and make the first throw. There are very many ways in which the advantage can be sought and/or gained.

One thing that should be stressed at the outset is that no matter whether you are throwing or working on your groundwork, there is one golden rule: **maximum efficiency: minimum effort**.

Judo, like most sports, requires you to limber up before you get started. There is nothing worse than going into any form of physical exercise with 'cold' muscles. So, to get them warmed up, spend five or ten minutes carrying out the illustrated leg, arm and back stretching exercises to get your body ready for the rigours of judo.

# JUDO

*Learning to fall is very important and something you should practise at a very early stage. You can always practise on your own, you don't need anybody to throw you.*

Before looking at the throws, you ought to learn how to fall properly because, believe me, you are going to receive some falls during your judo career.

The correct name for breaking your fall is *ukemi* (broken-fall). Your body should be relaxed and not tense as you fall. Your free arm should be outstretched and beat the mat on falling. A look at the examples show the correct ways to fall.

*In the example opposite your opponent is about to turn you over by dragging your right arm under you. You must be ready for the fall on to your back.*

*Notice how the left arm is brought to safety and out on to the mat. This will not only break the fall but will give you a free arm to help with any counter move.*

# TECHNIQUE

*Through this example you can learn to break your fall. As soon as your back hits the ground make sure your left arm is outstretched on to the mat, ready to push you back up on to your feet.*

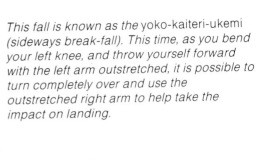

# JUDO

*This fall is known as the yoko-kaiteri-ukemi (sideways break-fall). This time, as you bend your left knee, and throw yourself forward with the left arm outstretched, it is possible to turn completely over and use the outstretched right arm to help take the impact on landing.*

# THROWS

The following throws have all been laid down by the British Judo Association in its Junior Grading System.

## O-GOSHI (Hip throw)

One of the basic throws, it is performed by lifting your opponent over your hip and as you move to the left side he is thrown over your right hip and on to the mat. As you grip your opponent around the back and under the arm, you will have your back to him and with your knees bent. As you straighten your knees and bend your trunk forward, that movement will bring your opponent up and over your hip.

### O-goshi

*This is an ideal throw for beginners because it gives them the feel of the hip throw which can be adapted into similar throws at a later stage.*

*Make sure you turn and put your back into your opponent's chest.*

*Bend forward pulling on your opponent's right arm and at the same time pulling on his back with your right arm.*

*Complete the throw by rolling your opponent over your hip.*

# JUDO

**Ko-uchi-gari**

*An effective sweep which can easily put your opponent on his back if taken unaware.*

*Holding your opponent with your right hand at his left lapel and left hand at the left elbow, sweep your right foot behind his heel.*

*Make sure it is the sole of your foot which contacts the heel. It is not a 'kick' but a 'sweep'.*

*Push forward as your opponent loses balance ready to commence your groundwork.*

# TECHNIQUE

### KO-UCHI-GARI (Inner reaping throw)

Performed by stepping forward and with your right foot placed behind your opponent's right heel so that the sole of your foot makes contact with his heel. Pull your foot sharply towards you. As your opponent falls backwards drive the upper body back at the same time. Don't attempt to lift him off the ground – his momentum will carry him down. As your opponent falls backwards he will invariably still be holding on to your *judogi* and you will be pulled to the mat with him but you will have the advantage and should be thinking of your next move once on the mat as you press for the hold or submission.

### IPPON-SEOI-NAGE (One arm shoulder throw)

Having grabbed one of your opponent's arms you should turn your back into him. Get your right shoulder under his right arm-pit, bend down and pull your opponent's arm forward. Your opponent will then be thrown over your back and onto the mat.

### Ippon-seoi-nage

*Regarded as the typical judo throw. Because you are lifting your opponent onto your back and then throwing him over your shoulder, it is more effective by the smaller fighter against a taller one because the centre of gravity of the taller man is higher.*

*Turn into your opponent with your back against his body. Ensure his right elbow is grabbed by your left hand and the right upper arm is locked by your right arm. Notice how your legs should be bent.*

*Now straighten your legs, this will have the effect of hauling him onto your back.*

*To complete the throw pull your right arm across your chest.*

## O-uchi-gari

*Major inner reaping using the heel to take your opponent off balance.*

*Pull your heel towards his foot and this will effect the unbalancing.*

## O-UCHI-GARI (Inner reaping throw)

A similar throw to the *ko-uchi-gari* but this time the back of your heel makes contact with the back of your opponent's leg around the calf area. There is less chance of your opponent grabbing your jacket as he falls to the mat because he is taken more off balance than with the *ko-uchi-gari*.

## TAI-OTOSHI (Body drop)

A form of hip throw but it is more of a drop than a throw. You don't grip your opponent around the back, as in the *o-goshi*, but instead grab hold of the left lapel and right sleeve.

*Step slightly to the side of your opponent and position your heel around the back of his lower leg.*

*As your opponent falls, drive into him ready to gain the advantage once on the mat.*

# TECHNIQUE

**Tai-otoshi**
An effective throw by a smaller fighter
against a bigger one because timing, rather
than strength, is important and if carried out
correctly is very effective.

From a normal face-on position, turn your
side into your opponent keeping your right
leg outstretched.

Pull your opponent across your outstretched
leg by pulling on the left arm and turning
your body to the left.

Complete the throw by driving your
opponent onto the mat.

### O-soto-gari

*The newcomer will find this move an easy one to carry out. You don't have to turn into your opponent and can effect it face-on.*

*Move slightly to the side of your opponent and reap your right leg around the back of his right knee.*

## O-SOTO-GARI
## (Outer reaping throw)

Like the *o-uchi-gari* this is a reaping movement with your heel against your opponent's calf but this time, as you grab him take a step forward with your left foot which will unbalance your opponent. Then wrap your right leg around the calf of his right leg and pull your foot towards you.

## KO-SOTO-GARI
## (Outer reaping throw)

A minor outer reaping movement whereby you unbalance your opponent by sweeping your left sole across his right heel. But the movement must be done in conjunction with the hands and you should have a hold of your opponent's right sleeve. At the same time as using your foot you should also pull down with your left hand as part of the unbalancing movement.

*Move your body-weight onto your left leg and at the same time pull down on your opponent's left arm.*

*Continue the throw by driving with your right arm which is holding your opponent's lapel.*

Angelo Parisi making a successful throw.
He represented Great Britain at international level
before becoming a nationalized Frenchman. He won
the heavyweight gold medal and Open class silver at
the 1980 Moscow Olympics

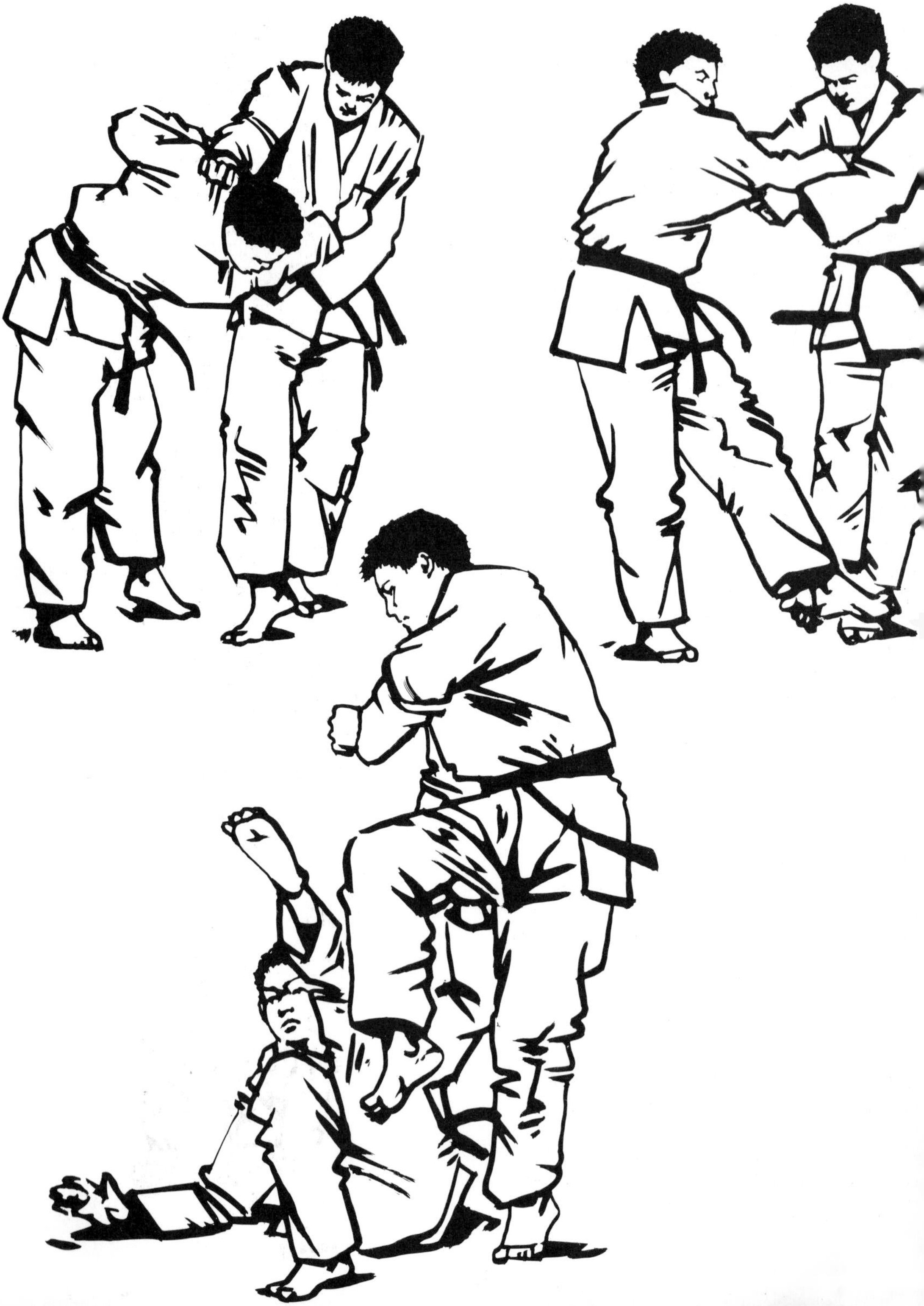

**Ko-soto-gari** *(left)*

*An ideal outer reaping throw when your opponent comes in to attack you from close quarters.*

*Drag him towards you and with the sole of your foot, sweep his left heel upwards.*

*The action is completed with the arms pulling and then pushing your opponent onto the mat. It is not only the feet which play a crucial role in moves like these, but the arms and hands are equally important. You must use your hands with good effect to make sure the unbalancing procedure is carried out properly.*

# MOROTE-SEOI-NAGE
## (Double arm shoulder throw)

Performed with your right hand gripping your opponent's left lapel and your left hand gripping the right sleeve at the elbow. Initially, you start by facing your opponent. You then make a full turn so your right shoulder goes into his chest. With a bent arm the movement is completed by curling the upper body downwards towards the mat, and your opponent will go over your shoulder.

**Morote-seoi-nage** *(right)*

*The two-armed shoulder throw is similar to the* ippon-seoi-nage *and is again effective for smaller fighters against taller opponents.*

*From a face-on position you turn your side into your opponent's chest and slightly bend your knees.*

*Grab your opponent's left lapel and right elbow and lift him/her onto your back.*

*With a straightening of the legs and pulling on the jacket your opponent is hauled over your right shoulder to the mat.*

### Tsuri-komi-goshi

*A form of the basic* o-goshi, *this move is a hip throw performed by lifting your opponent onto, and over, your hip.*

*Grab your opponent's right arm and pull him towards you.*

*Pivot on your right foot and turn your rear end beyond his right hip.*

## TSURI-KOMI-GOSHI (Lift-pull hip throw)

A hip throw with the opponent being lifted into the throw. The success of this throw depends on the feet. Move your right foot forwards about 30cm (1ft) in front of your left. Pivot on the ball of the leading foot and swing the left foot backwards to a point between your opponent's feet. At the same time, pull your opponent forward onto your hip with both hands. The straightening of your legs will complete the throw.

## HARAI-GOSHI (Sweeping hip throw)

Executed by gripping your opponent around the back of his collar and at the right elbow. From a position facing your opponent you make a full turn transferring your weight from your right leg and at the same time sweep your right leg up and across your opponent's thigh to carry out the throw.

**Harai-goshi** *(right)*
*The hip throw which employs a leg sweep to help carry out the throw.*

Keep hold of your opponent's right hand and be ready to start the groundwork.

Pull to the left with both hands and straighten your legs.

Break your opponent's balance by pulling on his left sleeve and get ready to pivot.

Turn your hip into his stomach so that your body is nearly parallel to the mat.

Sweep up your leg and pull down with both hands.

# JUDO

**Morote-seoi-otoshi**
*A combination of the one-arm shoulder throw* (morote-seoi-nage) *and body drop* (tai-otoshi).

With your back against your opponent's chest make sure your left knee is well bent and ready to take the pressure of the throw. Your right leg should be outstretched.

The lift is helped by pulling with both arms and bending your head forwards in the direction of the throw.

Keep hold of your opponent's right arm, then quickly get into position for the groundwork. Keep your left foot close to you, not too far out or the throw is too hard.

# TECHNIQUE

## MOROTE-SEOI-OTOSHI
(Shoulder drop)

Carried out by turning your body from a face-on position to a position with your back into your opponent. As you make the turn and transfer the weight to your left foot, your right leg comes up between your body and his. It is then outstretched and as you lean forward your opponent is dropped over your shoulder.

## SASAE-TSURIKOMI-ASHI
(Drawing ankle throw)

A throw making full use of your right foot. Having gripped your opponent around the elbow with your left hand, and lapel with the right hand (at approximately your shoulder height) you step forward with your right foot and turn it 90 degrees so your toes point towards your opponent's left foot. You transfer all your weight to your right foot and lift up your left one so that your sole is flat on the ground. Then, with a strong pulling movement with your left hand, turn your body to the left. This will throw your opponent forward.

**Sasae tsurikomi-ashi**
*An ankle sweep which is not as easy as it looks, and takes some practice before gaining perfection.*

*Get your opponent off balance by pulling down to his right.*

*Draw the sole of your left foot into his ankle.*

*Pulling with your left arm and pushing with the right will help to twist your opponent on to his back as he falls.*

# TECHNIQUE

## TSURI-KOMI-ASHI
## (Drawing Ankle)

A sweeping technique which needs some strength in the arms as your opponent falls right across your body to finish on the mat almost behind your start point. It is a good response to any attempt to pull and drag you without style on the mat, and combines well with *osoto-gari* for example.

### Okuri-ashi-barai

*Another sweeping ankle throw which involves the pulling and pushing of the arms before unbalancing your opponent.*

*Pull on your opponent's right sleeve and push on the left lapel to unbalance him.*

*As your opponent unbalances to the right, sweep with your left foot against his right ankle. But don't forget, use the sole of your foot and sweep, don't kick.*

*Push through with your leg and finish with a downward action to take your opponent over your left leg and over onto his back.*

**Britain's Karen Briggs on her way to another victory. She has dominated the extra-lightweight class in recent years.**

# JUDO

## Tomoe-nage

*A sacrifice throw whereby you forfeit your upright position to seek an advantage.*

*Raise your right foot towards the lower abdomen of your opponent but make sure your toes are pointing outwards, and not into the stomach.*

*Fall backwards on to the mat making sure your foot remains in the abdomen and also make sure you have a tight grip of your opponent.*

*The continuous movement will take your opponent over your head and into a breakfall position. Maintain the hold and get ready to start the groundwork.*

## TOMOE-NAGE (Stomach throw)

You step into your opponent with your left foot and then sit down on the mat in front of him, at the same time bringing your right foot up into his stomach at about belt height. Straighten the right leg and pull down on your opponent's jacket to ensure he goes over the top of you and lands on his back.

## TE-GURUMA (Hand wheel)

It is not easy to execute this throw but could well be a contest-winner if carried out properly. It is used as a counter attack. As your opponent comes forward, drop your centre of gravity by spreading and bending your legs. Grab his collar with your right hand and place your left hand between his legs grabbing the top of the thigh and then lift your opponent off the mat by straightening your legs. Complete the throw by pulling your opponent downwards with your right hand and up-ending him with your left. But, as your opponent falls, pull up sharply with your right hand to ensure he lands on his back.

**Te-guruma**

*A hand wheel normally executed as a counter attack. Once you have your opponent in this position, the throw is completed by pulling down with your right hand and turning him over with your left. To complete the turn on to his back, pull sharply with your right hand as your opponent is falling.*

**Morote-gari**
*A whole body scoop, grasping above
your opponents knees.*

## MOROTE-GARI
## (Two-handed scoop)

An attack on your opponent's knees, by
scooping him backwards onto the mat. The
attack is made by stepping forward with your
right foot, bending both knees and dropping
your body reaching around the back of your
opponent's legs and grabbing the backs of
his knees with your palms. Straighten your
legs and drive with your shoulders and drag
your opponent's legs towards you to
complete the throw.

*Move your right foot forward. Bend your
knees and trunk and grab your opponent
with the palms of your hands behind his
knees. This should automatically cause your
opponent to overbalance.*

*To continue the movement pull your hands
towards you and start moving into an
upright position.*

**Tani-otoshi**
*Another sacrifice throw, known as the Valley drop.*
*Having been in an upright position you slide to the mat with your*
*leg outstretched, over which you will drop your opponent. The*
*secret of this throw's success is in the hands once more. You must*
*push on the left lapel and pull the right elbow as your opponent*
*falls backwards. Keep alert because you will have an ideal*
*opportunity to gain a quick advantage on the groundwork after*
*completing the throw.*

## TANI-OTOSHI (Valley drop)

With a normal two-handed grip (the right
hand on your opponent's lapel and the other
on the left sleeve) lunge forward falling
towards the mat. As you hit the mat your
right leg should be outstretched and catch
behind your opponent's heels. Push your
weight to your right side, so that your
opponent falls backwards.

## UCHI-MATA (Inner thigh throw)

Adopt the normal grip (right hand on lapel,
left hand on sleeve) and pivot on your right
foot. As you complete the turn, transfer your
weight to your left foot and bring your right
leg up between your opponent's legs,
making contact with the top of the inside of
his thigh. Continue the movement until the
right leg is outstretched, so that your
opponent is lifted into the air and spun over
on to his back.

*You first unbalance your opponent to his right and then bring back your left foot some 50cm (18in) from its original forward position.*

*Turn to the left placing your left foot into the position occupied by your right foot, and sweep upwards with your right leg.*

You will probably have realized that in a lot of the throws we have covered, the fighter being thrown still has hold of the thrower. Consequently, the thrower will also fall to the ground. But in some cases the thrower will deliberately fall to the ground with his opponent in order to quickly attack while his opponent is on the ground. This is known as *maki-komi*.

There are occasions, however, when you will make a sacrifice throw (a *sutemi-waza*) and you will forfeit your own standing position to go down onto the mat with your opponent as you carry out the throw. This will enable you to gain a quick advantage when you start the groundwork. The *tani-otoshi* and *tomoe-nage* on the previous pages are good examples of sacrifice throws.

What we have taught you here is the basic throws from the point of view of the thrower. If you are on the receiving end it is important to make sure you land properly and safely. But is must be remembered that not all attacking movements are successful. It is possible for a throw to be blocked and, as the intended thrower is caught off guard, he is thrown himself. So, beware! And don't forget, a throw directly on to the back is an *ippon* and the contest is won – or lost –

### Uchi-mata

*An inner thigh reaping throw which is effective if carried out properly. But the big problem is maintaining your own balance. You have been warned!*

*To get extra lift, straighten your left supporting leg and to complete the throw, jerk with your right hip. Your opponent will turn over and onto the mat.*

*Make sure you retain a grip on your opponent's sleeve and are in a position to capitalize on your throwing technique by getting in some good groundwork.*

accordingly. It is therefore good practice to learn from a very early stage in your development, that when falling you should not land on your back.

The throws illustrated in this book, as well as others, all play a significant part in making winning scores. It is possible to get an *ippon* from the throws by making the perfect throw. But if that doesn't come off, then you have a chance, as a result of making the successful throw, of following up with a grapple good enought to win the points by either a submission or a successful pinning to the mat of your opponent.

However, you must always bear in mind

that your opponent is not going to stand there and let you carry out the throw of your choice. He is going to offer resistance. You must therefore always have a contingency plan in mind and the example overleaf shows how you can change your intended throw as a result of defensive action from your opponent. In this case, you have changed from a *ko-uchi-gari* to a *tai-otoshi*.

*Having decided on a ko-uchi-gari you may suddenly find you have to change your plans because your opponent, on seeing your move, has taken avoiding action.*

*So, quickly change your plans and attack with a* tai-otoshi.

# GRAPPLING

We will now look at some of the grappling techniques. Again they are as laid down in accordance with the BJA guidelines for junior boys and girls.

## KESA-GATAME (Scarf hold)

Adopt a sitting position, taking up the space between your opponent's right arm pit and his body which you will have created by taking his right arm and locking it under your left arm pit. Your right arm is then wrapped around your opponent's neck. Having taken up this position spread your legs to give you a firmer grip.

# TECHNIQUE

### Kesa-gatame
*The scarf hold is the most popular form of hold-down techniques.*

*Above: With your right arm around the back of your opponent's neck.*

*Below: With the right arm gripping tightly on his left shoulder.*

*In both cases your opponent's right arm is secured against your body.*

## KAMI-SHIHO-GATAME
## (Upper four quarters)

Grip your opponent's belt on both sides with your arms tucked well under his shoulders. Place your chest on his and rest your head to one side of the lower chest. Spread your knees to enable you to apply pressure.

**Kami-shiho-gatame**

*A hold-down technique applied if you find yourself above your opponent's head and he is lying face upwards on the mat.*

*It can be applied by stretching your body lengthwise on the mat and pushing with your toes to apply pressure, or . . .*

*. . . with your knees brought close to your opponent's head so that you are in a kneeling position.*

*In both cases you apply pressure on the chest with your head and secure the arms by placing your own arms under his and gripping his belt.*

## YOKO-SHIHO-GATAME
## (Side four quarters)

Similar to the *kami-shiho-gatame* but this time you adopt a position at right angles to your opponent. Your start position is with your knees apart and pressed against the side of your opponent's body. Pass your right hand under your opponent's neck and grab the collar. Then pass your right hand between his legs to grab his belt. Now exert strong body contact either by holding your knees against your opponent's body or by stretching your legs outwards and lowering your stomach to the mat.

**Yoko-shiho-gatame**
*A side four-quarter hold with several variants.*

*The standard hold. Your body is at right angles to your opponent's. First slide your right hand under his collar and grip his lapel. Then slide your left hand between his legs and underneath the back of his right leg to grip the belt. At the same time keep your own legs wide apart and feet raised ready to apply pressure by pushing forwards.*

*In this variant your right arm is not under the opponent's collar but around his right shoulder and your left is grabbing the back of his right leg. The pressure is applied by outstretching your left leg in between his two legs and pushing downwards with your head.*

# JUDO

**Kata-gatame**

*The secret is to first immobilize your opponent's free arm, the right in this case. You do that by pushing your body against it and then wrapping your right arm around your opponent's neck and securing the grip by taking hold of your left hand which you slide under his shoulder.*

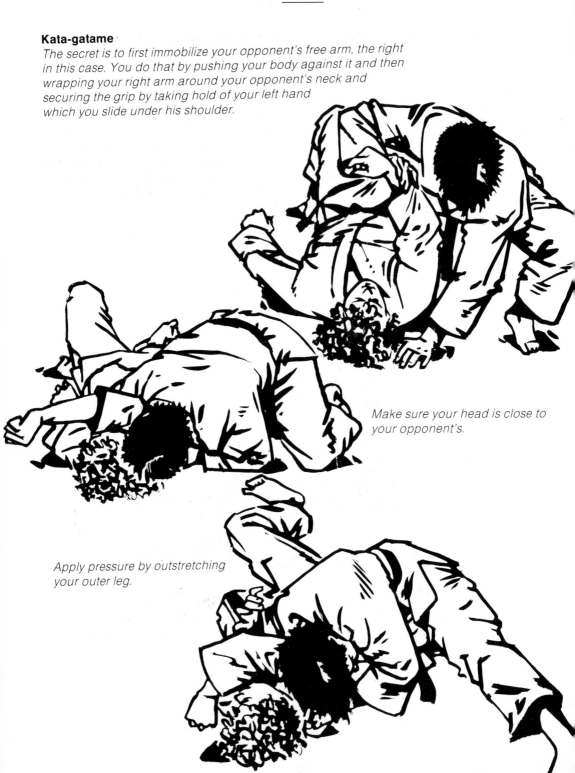

*Make sure your head is close to your opponent's.*

*Apply pressure by outstretching your outer leg.*

# TECHNIQUE

## KATA-GATAME (Shoulder holding)

Take up a kneeling position alongside your opponent. He will inevitably raise his right arm as a defensive movement. When your opponent does this push his elbow so his arm goes across his face. Wrap your right arm around his neck and then lower your head until it is touching the back of this hand. Now put your two hands together in a monkey grip and pull. At the same time lower your head further so it nearly touches the mat. Your opponent's right arm will be wedged between your head and his.

## USHIRO-KESA-GATAME (Reverse scarf hold)

Having taken up a sitting position alongside your opponent's head, spread your legs well apart and lie across his chest with your head facing towards his legs and feet. Grab the belt by passing your right hand under your opponent's right shoulder. Take the left arm out of play by tightly gripping the wrist under your left armpit and grab the sleeve with your hand. Make sure you spread your legs wide.

**Ushiro-kesa-gatame**
*The reverse scarf hold which is very difficult to escape from because you immobilize both your opponent's arms. Note the spreading of your legs to provide the necessary balance.*

## TATE-SHIHO-GATAME
## (Lengthwise four quarters)

Lie on top of your opponent with stomachs touching. Tightly lock your legs under his upper leg or buttocks. Use your left arm to force your opponent's right arm across his face by pushing at the elbow and then holding it in place by using the back of your neck. Place your right arm under his neck and grab the right shoulder, or get hold of your own left hand, if you can.

This time don't forget that your opponent isn't going to lie there while you get the necessary hold to win the match. He is going to attempt to wriggle out of the situation. You must always be prepared for this and be in a position ready to regain the advantage by adopting a different grappling technique.

**Tate-shiho-gatame**

*Applied when you find yourself straddling your opponent's chest, this move is known as the lengthwise four quarters hold or the trunk hold.*

*From a straddle position tuck your knees into your opponent's ribs.*

*Bend forward and slide your left arm under your opponent's neck and secure the hold by grabbing your own right wrist. Instinctively your opponent will try to lift his body to throw you off. But to maintain your position you should securely wrap your legs around the backs of your opponent's thighs.*

# GAINING · SUBMISSION

And now for some grappling techniques likely to produce a submission:

## UDE-GARAMI (Entangled arm lock)

Lie across your opponent from a right angle position and place your chest on his. Take the left wrist in your left hand. Pass your right arm under his left arm and grab the wrist of your left hand. Raise your right arm and entire right side of your body so that you look towards your opponent's feet. This will cause a jerking movement and produce a likely submission as you turn his arms towards the mat.

**Ude-garami**
*The entangled arm lock. This diagram shows the position of your two arms in order to gain the maximum leverage.*

## Juji-gatame

*The cross arm lock. It is an ideal grappling technique to follow-up after a throw if you are still holding on to your opponent's arm.*

*Step over your opponent's neck with your left foot, and at the same time secure his right wrist with both hands and pull the arm upwards.*

*Fall backwards onto the mat maintaining the grip on the right wrist. A submission shouldn't be too far away!*

## JUJI-GATAME (Cross arm lock)

Take hold of your opponent's outstretched right hand grabbing the wrist with both your hands. At the same time, take up a seated position on the floor and pass your legs across his face and securely lock the outstretched arms between your legs. Don't jerk your opponent's arm to try to get the submission but gently pull it towards you. If necessary, apply more pressure by raising your hips. Make sure your opponent's left thumb is pointing upwards.

## WAKI-GATAME (Arm-pit hold)

Having got your opponent face down on the mat, take up a sitting position with your back leaning against his and with his left arm outstretched grip the wrist with both of your hands. To gain the submission, you apply pressure on your opponent's elbow by pushing down on the upper arm with your right arm-pit and, at the same time, lever his forearm upwards.

**Waki-gatame**

*The arm-pit hold. It is best performed during groundwork, as shown, but can also be applied with both fighters standing up. The pressure is applied by twisting your opponent's wrist and at the same time pulling his arm upwards and pressing downwards with your arm-pit onto the elbow joint. A submission should, again be not too far away.*

# JUDO

## UDE-GATAME (Straight arm lock)

Having taken up a kneeling position close to your opponent's right shoulder, he will instinctively push his right arm up to fend you off. As this happens grab your opponent's elbow from behind with your right hand and overlap your left hand over your right. Make sure his left hand is placed alongside your neck. Now pull his/her elbow towards you until he submits . . . hopefully!

## NAMI-JUJI-JIME (Cross arm strangle)

Grip the inside of your opponent's collar with both hands, but crossed. Pull the head downwards towards your chest to apply the pressure on his neck. Make sure you pull your elbows out of the way to enable the full movement of your opponent's head.

**Ude-gatame**

*Straight arm lock, or sometimes referred to as the arm crush. It can be applied at any time during a contest when your opponent 'offers' you an open arm. Quite simply, you apply pressure at the back of the elbow and pull towards your own body. Unless he can get out of it then a submission will almost certainly follow.*

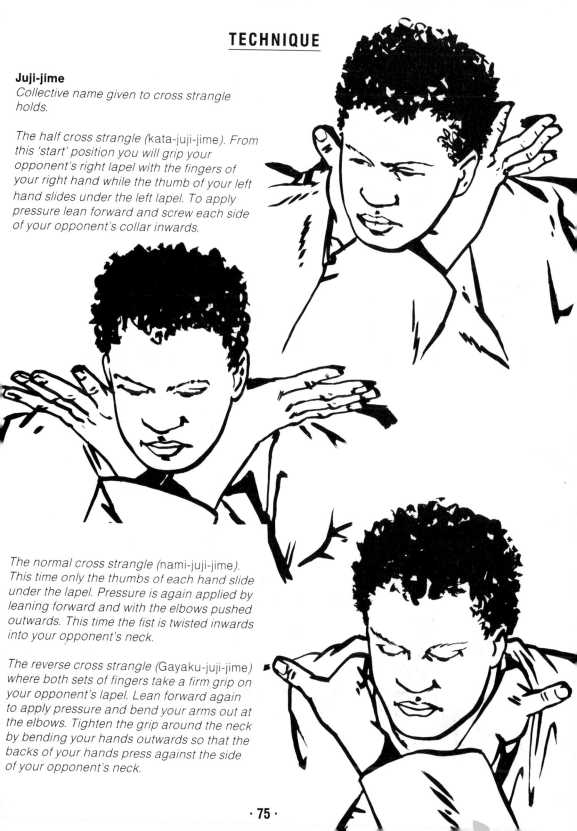

## Juji-jime
Collective name given to cross strangle holds.

The half cross strangle (kata-juji-jime). From this 'start' position you will grip your opponent's right lapel with the fingers of your right hand while the thumb of your left hand slides under the left lapel. To apply pressure lean forward and screw each side of your opponent's collar inwards.

The normal cross strangle (nami-juji-jime). This time only the thumbs of each hand slide under the lapel. Pressure is again applied by leaning forward and with the elbows pushed outwards. This time the fist is twisted inwards into your opponent's neck.

The reverse cross strangle (Gayaku-juji-jime) where both sets of fingers take a firm grip on your opponent's lapel. Lean forward again to apply pressure and bend your arms out at the elbows. Tighten the grip around the neck by bending your hands outwards so that the backs of your hands press against the side of your opponent's neck.

## OKURI-ERI-JIME
## (Sliding collar lock)

From a position behind your opponent, slide your left hand between his left arm and body and grip the left lapel of his suit and pull downwards. Place your right arm across your opponent's neck and grip the left collar as high as possible. To now go for the submission, straighten your two arms rather than pull them outwards.

### Okuri-eri-jime

*The sliding collar strangle. It can be effective because it enables you to apply pressure to both the throat and side of the neck at the same time. If you are carrying it out as part of your groundwork then you can help secure the hold by wrapping your legs around your opponent's trunk.*

### Kata-ha-jime

*The single wing neck lock. It is normally applied when you are in a kneeling position behind your opponent.*

# TECHNIQUE

## KATA-HA-JIME (Single wing neck lock)

Kneeling behind your opponent, place your right hand under his chin and grip the upper part of the left lapel. Place your left arm across the back of your opponent's neck but with his left arm lifted up and locked between your arm and your chest. To now apply the necessary pressure, pull with the right hand and push with your left forearm.

## HADAKE-JIME (Naked strangle)

Again adopt a kneeling position behind your opponent. Place your right arm across his throat. Place your left hand over his left shoulder and grab your right hand. Pull your

right hand towards you, making sure the one just above your right wrist is pressing into your opponent's throat.

Right, that's it on basic grappling techniques. But one thing we cannot stress too strongly is once you have obtained a submission, release the pressure on your opponent.

All the throwing and grappling techniques have been shown from one side of the body or the other. They can, of course, be effected the opposite way around, in which case reference to right arm, right leg, etc, should be reversed.

The techniques outlined are the basic ones you will need to learn as a newcomer to judo. There are other techniques, and indeed there are varieties of the ones shown, but these will be learned as you develop and gain more experience. The techniques outlined are purely to give you an introduction to them. For your further development you must go to a judo club approved by the British Judo Association, or some other national association if you live outside Britain. The addresses of major organizations can be found at the end of the book. If you want to know how to join a club, or where the nearest one is to you, contact your appropriate national association, they will be only too pleased to help.

Judo is fun and there is no age barrier. The younger you can get started the better. There is no sexual discrimination either. It is a sport for women and girls; not just men and boys. So, men, women, boys and girls go out and enjoy judo. We hope that through *Play the Game* we have given you a sound basic introduction to the sport.

**Hadake-jime**
*The naked strangle hold, so called because you make no use of your opponent's jacket when applying the hold. Again, it is normally made from a kneeling position behind your opponent.*

# USEFUL
# ADDRESSES

There are many judo clubs across the country and there will be one not too far away from you. For details of your nearest club, contact the relevant address below and they will be only too pleased to put you in touch with them.

**British Judo Association**
9 Islington High Street
London N1 9LQ
01-833 4424

**British Schools Judo Association**
21 Finborough Road
Tooting
London SW17 9HY
01-640 6083

**International Judo Federation**
PSF 380 RDA
106 Berlin
East Germany
37-2-2291633

# RULES CLINIC

# INDEX

# INDEX